CHRISTMAS
Party Planner

NAME: _____

PHONE: _____

DEDICATION

This Christmas Party Planner Book is dedicated to all the Christmas enthusiasts out there who want to plan a Christmas party and document their findings in the process.

You are my inspiration for producing books and I'm honored to be a part of keeping all of your Christmas party planning notes and records organized.

This journal notebook will help you record the details of your party planning.

Thoughtfully put together with these sections to record: Date, Time, Location, # of Guests, Budget, Theme, Dress Code, Kids Invited?, Schedule, To Do, Activities & Games, and Roles.

HOW TO USE THIS BOOK

The purpose of this book is to keep all of your Christmas party planning notes all in one place. It will help keep you organized.

This Christmas Party Planner Book will allow you to accurately document every detail about your Christmas party planning.

Here are examples of the prompts for you to fill in and write about your experience in this book:

1. Location
2. Date
3. Time
4. Number of Guests
5. Budget
6. Theme
7. Dress Code
8. Kids Invited?
9. Schedule
10. To Do
11. Activities & Games
12. Roles

CHRISTMAS *Party Planner*

LOCATION:

DATE:

TIME:

NO. OF GUESTS

BUDGET:

THEME

DRESS CODE

KIDS INVITE

YES   NO

SCHEDULE

TO-DOS

- [ ]
- [ ]
- [ ]
- [ ]
- [ ]
- [ ]
- [ ]
- [ ]
- [ ]
- [ ]
- [ ]
- [ ]
- [ ]
- [ ]
- [ ]

ACTIVITIES / GAMES

ROLES

CHRISTMAS *Party Planner*

LOCATION:

DATE:

TIME:

NO. OF GUESTS

BUDGET:

THEME	DRESS CODE	KIDS INVITE
		◯ YES ◯ NO

SCHEDULE

TO-DOS

- ☐
- ☐
- ☐
- ☐
- ☐
- ☐
- ☐
- ☐
- ☐
- ☐
- ☐
- ☐
- ☐

ACTIVITIES / GAMES

- ◯
- ◯
- ◯
- ◯
- ◯
- ◯

ROLES

CHRISTMAS *Party Planner*

LOCATION: **DATE:**

TIME: **NO. OF GUESTS**   **BUDGET:**

THEME   **DRESS CODE**   **KIDS INVITE**

YES   NO

SCHEDULE

TO-DOS

- [ ]
- [ ]
- [ ]
- [ ]
- [ ]
- [ ]
- [ ]
- [ ]
- [ ]
- [ ]
- [ ]
- [ ]
- [ ]

ACTIVITIES / GAMES

ROLES

CHRISTMAS *Party Planner*

LOCATION: DATE:

TIME: NO. OF GUESTS   BUDGET:

THEME	DRESS CODE	KIDS INVITE
		○ YES NO

SCHEDULE

TO-DOS

☐
☐
☐
☐
☐
☐
☐
☐
☐
☐
☐
☐
☐
☐

ACTIVITIES / GAMES

ROLES

CHRISTMAS *Party Planner*

LOCATION: DATE:

TIME: NO. OF GUESTS   BUDGET:

THEME   DRESS CODE   KIDS INVITE

                                                    ◯ YES   ◯ NO

SCHEDULE

TO-DOS

☐
☐
☐
☐
☐
☐
☐
☐
☐
☐
☐
☐
☐

ACTIVITIES / GAMES   **ROLES**

CHRISTMAS *Party Planner*

LOCATION:		DATE:	

TIME:		NO. OF GUESTS		BUDGET:	

THEME	DRESS CODE	KIDS INVITE
		◯ YES ◯ NO

SCHEDULE

TO-DOS

- ☐
- ☐
- ☐
- ☐
- ☐
- ☐
- ☐
- ☐
- ☐
- ☐
- ☐
- ☐
- ☐
- ☐

ACTIVITIES / GAMES

ROLES

CHRISTMAS *Party Planner*

LOCATION:

DATE:

TIME:

NO. OF GUESTS

BUDGET:

THEME

DRESS CODE

KIDS INVITE

YES   NO

SCHEDULE

TO-DOS

☐
☐
☐
☐
☐
☐
☐
☐
☐
☐
☐
☐
☐
☐

ACTIVITIES / GAMES

ROLES

CHRISTMAS *Party Planner*

LOCATION:

DATE:

TIME:

NO. OF GUESTS

BUDGET:

THEME	DRESS CODE	KIDS INVITE
		○ YES ○ NO

SCHEDULE

TO-DOS

☐
☐
☐
☐
☐
☐
☐
☐
☐
☐
☐
☐
☐

ACTIVITIES / GAMES

ROLES

CHRISTMAS *Party Planner*

LOCATION: | DATE:

TIME: | NO. OF GUESTS | BUDGET:

THEME	DRESS CODE	KIDS INVITE
		○ YES ○ NO

SCHEDULE

TO-DOS

☐
☐
☐
☐
☐
☐
☐
☐
☐
☐
☐
☐
☐
☐

ACTIVITIES / GAMES

ROLES

CHRISTMAS *Party Planner*

LOCATION:

DATE:

TIME:

NO. OF GUESTS

BUDGET:

THEME	DRESS CODE	KIDS INVITE
		○ YES ○ NO

SCHEDULE

TO-DOS

☐
☐
☐
☐
☐
☐
☐
☐
☐
☐
☐
☐
☐

ACTIVITIES / GAMES

○
○
○
○
○
○
○
○

ROLES

CHRISTMAS *Party Planner*

LOCATION: DATE:

TIME: NO. OF GUESTS   BUDGET:

THEME   DRESS CODE   KIDS INVITE

                                                              YES   NO

SCHEDULE		TO-DOS
		☐
		☐
		☐
		☐
		☐
		☐
		☐
		☐
		☐
		☐
		☐
		☐
		☐
		☐

         ACTIVITIES / GAMES   ROLES

CHRISTMAS *Party Planner*

LOCATION:

DATE:

TIME:

NO. OF GUESTS

BUDGET:

THEME

DRESS CODE

KIDS INVITE

⭕ YES ⭕ NO

SCHEDULE

TO-DOS

☐
☐
☐
☐
☐
☐
☐
☐
☐
☐
☐
☐
☐

ACTIVITIES / GAMES

ROLES

CHRISTMAS *Party Planner*

LOCATION:

DATE:

TIME:

NO. OF GUESTS

BUDGET:

THEME

DRESS CODE

KIDS INVITE

YES   NO

SCHEDULE

TO-DOS

- [ ]
- [ ]
- [ ]
- [ ]
- [ ]
- [ ]
- [ ]
- [ ]
- [ ]
- [ ]
- [ ]
- [ ]
- [ ]
- [ ]

ACTIVITIES / GAMES

ROLES

CHRISTMAS *Party Planner*

LOCATION:		DATE:

TIME:	NO. OF GUESTS	BUDGET:

THEME	DRESS CODE	KIDS INVITE
		◯ YES ◯ NO

SCHEDULE

TO-DOS

☐
☐
☐
☐
☐
☐
☐
☐
☐
☐
☐
☐
☐
☐

ACTIVITIES / GAMES

ROLES

CHRISTMAS *Party Planner*

LOCATION: **DATE:**

TIME: **NO. OF GUESTS**   **BUDGET:**

THEME   **DRESS CODE**   **KIDS INVITE**

                                                              YES   NO

SCHEDULE

TO-DOS

- [ ]
- [ ]
- [ ]
- [ ]
- [ ]
- [ ]
- [ ]
- [ ]
- [ ]
- [ ]
- [ ]
- [ ]
- [ ]
- [ ]

ACTIVITIES / GAMES   **ROLES**

CHRISTMAS *Party Planner*

LOCATION:

DATE:

TIME:

NO. OF GUESTS

BUDGET:

THEME

DRESS CODE

KIDS INVITE

○ YES   ○ NO

SCHEDULE

TO-DOS

☐
☐
☐
☐
☐
☐
☐
☐
☐
☐
☐
☐
☐
☐
☐

ACTIVITIES / GAMES

ROLES

CHRISTMAS *Party Planner*

LOCATION: **DATE:**

TIME: **NO. OF GUESTS**   **BUDGET:**

THEME	DRESS CODE	KIDS INVITE
		YES NO

SCHEDULE

TO-DOS

- [ ]
- [ ]
- [ ]
- [ ]
- [ ]
- [ ]
- [ ]
- [ ]
- [ ]
- [ ]
- [ ]
- [ ]
- [ ]
- [ ]

ACTIVITIES / GAMES

ROLES

CHRISTMAS *Party Planner*

LOCATION:

DATE:

TIME:

NO. OF GUESTS

BUDGET:

THEME

DRESS CODE

KIDS INVITE

○ YES ○ NO

SCHEDULE

TO-DOS

☐
☐
☐
☐
☐
☐
☐
☐
☐
☐
☐
☐
☐
☐

ACTIVITIES / GAMES

ROLES

CHRISTMAS *Party Planner*

LOCATION:

DATE:

TIME:

NO. OF GUESTS

BUDGET:

THEME

DRESS CODE

KIDS INVITE

YES   NO

SCHEDULE	

	TO-DOS
☐	
☐	
☐	
☐	
☐	
☐	
☐	
☐	
☐	
☐	
☐	
☐	
☐	
☐	
☐	

ACTIVITIES / GAMES

ROLES

CHRISTMAS *Party Planner*

LOCATION:

DATE:

TIME:

NO. OF GUESTS

BUDGET:

THEME

DRESS CODE

KIDS INVITE

◯ YES ◯ NO

SCHEDULE

TO-DOS

☐
☐
☐
☐
☐
☐
☐
☐
☐
☐
☐
☐
☐

ACTIVITIES / GAMES

ROLES

CHRISTMAS *Party Planner*

LOCATION:

DATE:

TIME:

NO. OF GUESTS

BUDGET:

THEME

DRESS CODE

KIDS INVITE

◯ YES   ◯ NO

SCHEDULE

TO-DOS

☐
☐
☐
☐
☐
☐
☐
☐
☐
☐
☐
☐
☐
☐

ACTIVITIES / GAMES

ROLES

CHRISTMAS *Party Planner*

LOCATION:

DATE:

TIME:

NO. OF GUESTS

BUDGET:

THEME

DRESS CODE

KIDS INVITE

◯ YES   ◯ NO

SCHEDULE

TO-DOS

☐
☐
☐
☐
☐
☐
☐
☐
☐
☐
☐
☐
☐

ACTIVITIES / GAMES

ROLES

◯
◯
◯
◯
◯

CHRISTMAS *Party Planner*

LOCATION:

DATE:

TIME:

NO. OF GUESTS

BUDGET:

THEME

DRESS CODE

KIDS INVITE

YES   NO

SCHEDULE

TO-DOS

- [ ]
- [ ]
- [ ]
- [ ]
- [ ]
- [ ]
- [ ]
- [ ]
- [ ]
- [ ]
- [ ]
- [ ]
- [ ]

ACTIVITIES / GAMES

ROLES

CHRISTMAS *Party Planner*

LOCATION:

DATE:

TIME:

NO. OF GUESTS

BUDGET:

THEME

DRESS CODE

KIDS INVITE

○ YES ○ NO

SCHEDULE

TO-DOS

☐
☐
☐
☐
☐
☐
☐
☐
☐
☐
☐
☐
☐

ACTIVITIES / GAMES

ROLES

○
○
○
○
○
○

CHRISTMAS *Party Planner*

LOCATION:

DATE:

TIME:

NO. OF GUESTS

BUDGET:

THEME	DRESS CODE	KIDS INVITE
		YES NO

SCHEDULE

TO-DOS

- [ ]
- [ ]
- [ ]
- [ ]
- [ ]
- [ ]
- [ ]
- [ ]
- [ ]
- [ ]
- [ ]
- [ ]
- [ ]

ACTIVITIES / GAMES

ROLES

CHRISTMAS *Party Planner*

LOCATION:

DATE:

TIME:

NO. OF GUESTS

BUDGET:

THEME	DRESS CODE	KIDS INVITE
		○ YES ○ NO

SCHEDULE

TO-DOS

- [ ]
- [ ]
- [ ]
- [ ]
- [ ]
- [ ]
- [ ]
- [ ]
- [ ]
- [ ]
- [ ]
- [ ]
- [ ]
- [ ]

ACTIVITIES / GAMES

ROLES

CHRISTMAS *Party Planner*

LOCATION:

DATE:

TIME:

NO. OF GUESTS

BUDGET:

THEME	DRESS CODE	KIDS INVITE
		YES NO

SCHEDULE

TO-DOS

- [ ]
- [ ]
- [ ]
- [ ]
- [ ]
- [ ]
- [ ]
- [ ]
- [ ]
- [ ]
- [ ]
- [ ]
- [ ]
- [ ]

ACTIVITIES / GAMES

ROLES

CHRISTMAS *Party Planner*

LOCATION:

DATE:

TIME:

NO. OF GUESTS

BUDGET:

THEME

DRESS CODE

KIDS INVITE

○ YES   ○ NO

SCHEDULE

TO-DOS

☐
☐
☐
☐
☐
☐
☐
☐
☐
☐
☐
☐
☐

ACTIVITIES / GAMES

ROLES

○
○
○
○
○
○

CHRISTMAS *Party Planner*

LOCATION:

DATE:

TIME:

NO. OF GUESTS

BUDGET:

THEME

DRESS CODE

KIDS INVITE

YES   NO

SCHEDULE

TO-DOS

- [ ]
- [ ]
- [ ]
- [ ]
- [ ]
- [ ]
- [ ]
- [ ]
- [ ]
- [ ]
- [ ]
- [ ]
- [ ]

ACTIVITIES / GAMES

ROLES

CHRISTMAS *Party Planner*

LOCATION:

DATE:

TIME:

NO. OF GUESTS

BUDGET:

THEME	DRESS CODE	KIDS INVITE
		○ YES ○ NO

SCHEDULE

TO-DOS

☐
☐
☐
☐
☐
☐
☐
☐
☐
☐
☐
☐
☐
☐

ACTIVITIES / GAMES

○
○
○
○
○
○

ROLES

CHRISTMAS *Party Planner*

LOCATION:

DATE:

TIME:

NO. OF GUESTS

BUDGET:

THEME

DRESS CODE

KIDS INVITE

YES   NO

SCHEDULE

TO-DOS

- [ ]
- [ ]
- [ ]
- [ ]
- [ ]
- [ ]
- [ ]
- [ ]
- [ ]
- [ ]
- [ ]
- [ ]
- [ ]
- [ ]

ACTIVITIES / GAMES

ROLES

CHRISTMAS *Party Planner*

LOCATION:

DATE:

TIME:

NO. OF GUESTS

BUDGET:

THEME

DRESS CODE

KIDS INVITE

◯ YES ◯ NO

SCHEDULE

TO-DOS

☐
☐
☐
☐
☐
☐
☐
☐
☐
☐
☐
☐
☐

ACTIVITIES / GAMES

ROLES

CHRISTMAS *Party Planner*

LOCATION: | DATE:

TIME: | NO. OF GUESTS | BUDGET:

THEME | DRESS CODE | KIDS INVITE
| | YES   NO

SCHEDULE	TO-DOS
	☐
	☐
	☐
	☐
	☐
	☐
	☐
	☐
	☐
	☐
	☐
	☐
	☐

ACTIVITIES / GAMES | **ROLES**

CHRISTMAS *Party Planner*

LOCATION: **DATE:**

TIME: **NO. OF GUESTS**   **BUDGET:**

THEME	DRESS CODE	KIDS INVITE
		◯ YES ◯ NO

SCHEDULE

TO-DOS

☐
☐
☐
☐
☐
☐
☐
☐
☐
☐
☐
☐
☐

ACTIVITIES / GAMES

◯
◯
◯
◯
◯
◯
◯

ROLES

CHRISTMAS *Party Planner*

LOCATION: **DATE:**

TIME: **NO. OF GUESTS**   **BUDGET:**

THEME   **DRESS CODE**   **KIDS INVITE**

YES   NO

SCHEDULE

TO-DOS

- [ ]
- [ ]
- [ ]
- [ ]
- [ ]
- [ ]
- [ ]
- [ ]
- [ ]
- [ ]
- [ ]
- [ ]
- [ ]

ACTIVITIES / GAMES   **ROLES**

CHRISTMAS *Party Planner*

| LOCATION: | | DATE: | |

| TIME: | | NO. OF GUESTS | | BUDGET: | |

THEME	DRESS CODE	KIDS INVITE
		○ YES ○ NO

SCHEDULE

TO-DOS

☐
☐
☐
☐
☐
☐
☐
☐
☐
☐
☐
☐
☐

ACTIVITIES / GAMES

○
○
○
○
○
○

ROLES

CHRISTMAS *Party Planner*

LOCATION:

DATE:

TIME:

NO. OF GUESTS

BUDGET:

THEME	DRESS CODE	KIDS INVITE
		○ YES ○ NO

SCHEDULE

TO-DOS

☐
☐
☐
☐
☐
☐
☐
☐
☐
☐
☐
☐
☐
☐
☐

ACTIVITIES / GAMES

ROLES

CHRISTMAS *Party Planner*

LOCATION:

DATE:

TIME:

NO. OF GUESTS

BUDGET:

THEME	DRESS CODE	KIDS INVITE
		○ YES ○ NO

SCHEDULE

TO-DOS

☐
☐
☐
☐
☐
☐
☐
☐
☐
☐
☐
☐
☐
☐

ACTIVITIES / GAMES

○
○
○
○
○
○
○

ROLES

CHRISTMAS *Party Planner*

LOCATION: DATE:

TIME: NO. OF GUESTS   BUDGET:

THEME	DRESS CODE	KIDS INVITE
		YES NO

SCHEDULE		TO-DOS	
		☐	
		☐	
		☐	
		☐	
		☐	
		☐	
		☐	
		☐	
		☐	
		☐	
		☐	
		☐	
		☐	
		☐	

ACTIVITIES / GAMES   **ROLES**

CHRISTMAS *Party Planner*

LOCATION: DATE:

TIME: NO. OF GUESTS   BUDGET:

THEME   DRESS CODE   KIDS INVITE

                                        ◯ YES   ◯ NO

SCHEDULE

TO-DOS

☐
☐
☐
☐
☐
☐
☐
☐
☐
☐
☐
☐
☐

ACTIVITIES / GAMES

ROLES

CHRISTMAS *Party Planner*

LOCATION:		DATE:
TIME:	NO. OF GUESTS	BUDGET:

THEME	DRESS CODE	KIDS INVITE
		◯ YES ◯ NO

SCHEDULE

TO-DOS

☐
☐
☐
☐
☐
☐
☐
☐
☐
☐
☐
☐
☐
☐
☐

ACTIVITIES / GAMES

ROLES

CHRISTMAS *Party Planner*

LOCATION:

DATE:

TIME:

NO. OF GUESTS

BUDGET:

THEME	DRESS CODE	KIDS INVITE
		○ YES ○ NO

SCHEDULE

TO-DOS

☐
☐
☐
☐
☐
☐
☐
☐
☐
☐
☐
☐
☐

ACTIVITIES / GAMES

○
○
○
○
○
○

ROLES

CHRISTMAS *Party Planner*

LOCATION: | DATE:

TIME: | NO. OF GUESTS | BUDGET:

THEME | DRESS CODE | KIDS INVITE

YES ◯ NO

SCHEDULE

TO-DOS

☐
☐
☐
☐
☐
☐
☐
☐
☐
☐
☐
☐
☐
☐

ACTIVITIES / GAMES

ROLES

CHRISTMAS *Party Planner*

LOCATION:

DATE:

TIME:

NO. OF GUESTS

BUDGET:

THEME	DRESS CODE	KIDS INVITE
		○ YES ○ NO

SCHEDULE

TO-DOS

- ☐
- ☐
- ☐
- ☐
- ☐
- ☐
- ☐
- ☐
- ☐
- ☐
- ☐
- ☐

ACTIVITIES / GAMES

ROLES

CHRISTMAS *Party Planner*

LOCATION: DATE:

TIME: NO. OF GUESTS   BUDGET:

THEME	DRESS CODE	KIDS INVITE
		◯ YES ◯ NO

SCHEDULE

TO-DOS

- ☐
- ☐
- ☐
- ☐
- ☐
- ☐
- ☐
- ☐
- ☐
- ☐
- ☐
- ☐
- ☐

ACTIVITIES / GAMES

ROLES

CHRISTMAS *Party Planner*

LOCATION:		DATE:	
TIME:	NO. OF GUESTS	BUDGET:	

THEME	DRESS CODE	KIDS INVITE
		○ YES ○ NO

SCHEDULE

TO-DOS

☐
☐
☐
☐
☐
☐
☐
☐
☐
☐
☐
☐
☐
☐

ACTIVITIES / GAMES

○
○
○
○
○

ROLES

CHRISTMAS *Party Planner*

LOCATION:

DATE:

TIME:

NO. OF GUESTS

BUDGET:

THEME	DRESS CODE	KIDS INVITE
		YES ○ NO ○

SCHEDULE

TO-DOS

☐
☐
☐
☐
☐
☐
☐
☐
☐
☐
☐
☐
☐

ACTIVITIES / GAMES

ROLES

CHRISTMAS *Party Planner*

LOCATION:

DATE:

TIME:

NO. OF GUESTS

BUDGET:

THEME	DRESS CODE	KIDS INVITE
		○ YES ○ NO

SCHEDULE

TO-DOS

☐
☐
☐
☐
☐
☐
☐
☐
☐
☐
☐
☐
☐

ACTIVITIES / GAMES

○
○
○
○
○
○

ROLES

CHRISTMAS *Party Planner*

LOCATION:

DATE:

TIME:

NO. OF GUESTS

BUDGET:

THEME

DRESS CODE

KIDS INVITE

◯ YES ◯ NO

SCHEDULE		TO-DOS
		☐
		☐
		☐
		☐
		☐
		☐
		☐
		☐
		☐
		☐
		☐
		☐
		☐
		☐

ACTIVITIES / GAMES

ROLES

CHRISTMAS *Party Planner*

LOCATION:

DATE:

TIME:

NO. OF GUESTS

BUDGET:

THEME	DRESS CODE	KIDS INVITE
		○ YES ○ NO

SCHEDULE

TO-DOS

- [ ]
- [ ]
- [ ]
- [ ]
- [ ]
- [ ]
- [ ]
- [ ]
- [ ]
- [ ]
- [ ]
- [ ]
- [ ]
- [ ]

ACTIVITIES / GAMES

ROLES

CHRISTMAS *Party Planner*

LOCATION:

DATE:

TIME:

NO. OF GUESTS

BUDGET:

THEME

DRESS CODE

KIDS INVITE

YES   NO

SCHEDULE

TO-DOS

- [ ]
- [ ]
- [ ]
- [ ]
- [ ]
- [ ]
- [ ]
- [ ]
- [ ]
- [ ]
- [ ]
- [ ]
- [ ]

ACTIVITIES / GAMES

ROLES

CHRISTMAS *Party Planner*

LOCATION:

DATE:

TIME:

NO. OF GUESTS

BUDGET:

THEME

DRESS CODE

KIDS INVITE

◯ YES ◯ NO

SCHEDULE

TO-DOS

☐
☐
☐
☐
☐
☐
☐
☐
☐
☐
☐
☐
☐

ACTIVITIES / GAMES

ROLES

CHRISTMAS *Party Planner*

LOCATION:

DATE:

TIME:

NO. OF GUESTS

BUDGET:

THEME

DRESS CODE

KIDS INVITE

YES   NO

SCHEDULE

TO-DOS

- [ ]
- [ ]
- [ ]
- [ ]
- [ ]
- [ ]
- [ ]
- [ ]
- [ ]
- [ ]
- [ ]
- [ ]
- [ ]

ACTIVITIES / GAMES

ROLES

CHRISTMAS *Party Planner*

LOCATION:

DATE:

TIME:

NO. OF GUESTS

BUDGET:

THEME

DRESS CODE

KIDS INVITE

◯ YES　◯ NO

SCHEDULE

TO-DOS

☐
☐
☐
☐
☐
☐
☐
☐
☐
☐
☐
☐
☐

ACTIVITIES / GAMES

ROLES

CHRISTMAS *Party Planner*

LOCATION:

DATE:

TIME:

NO. OF GUESTS

BUDGET:

THEME

DRESS CODE

KIDS INVITE

YES   NO

SCHEDULE	TO-DOS
	☐
	☐
	☐
	☐
	☐
	☐
	☐
	☐
	☐
	☐
	☐
	☐

ACTIVITIES / GAMES

ROLES

CHRISTMAS *Party Planner*

LOCATION:

DATE:

TIME:

NO. OF GUESTS

BUDGET:

THEME	DRESS CODE	KIDS INVITE
		○ YES ○ NO

SCHEDULE

TO-DOS

☐
☐
☐
☐
☐
☐
☐
☐
☐
☐
☐
☐
☐

ACTIVITIES / GAMES

○
○
○
○
○
○

ROLES

CHRISTMAS *Party Planner*

LOCATION: **DATE:**

TIME: **NO. OF GUESTS**   **BUDGET:**

THEME	DRESS CODE	KIDS INVITE
		YES NO

SCHEDULE	TO-DOS
	☐
	☐
	☐
	☐
	☐
	☐
	☐
	☐
	☐
	☐
	☐
	☐

ACTIVITIES / GAMES   **ROLES**

CHRISTMAS *Party Planner*

LOCATION: | DATE:

TIME: | NO. OF GUESTS | BUDGET:

THEME	DRESS CODE	KIDS INVITE
		◯ YES ◯ NO

SCHEDULE

TO-DOS

☐
☐
☐
☐
☐
☐
☐
☐
☐
☐
☐
☐
☐

ACTIVITIES / GAMES

ROLES

CHRISTMAS *Party Planner*

LOCATION:

DATE:

TIME:

NO. OF GUESTS

BUDGET:

THEME

DRESS CODE

KIDS INVITE

◯ YES ◯ NO

SCHEDULE

TO-DOS

☐
☐
☐
☐
☐
☐
☐
☐
☐
☐
☐
☐
☐
☐

ACTIVITIES / GAMES

ROLES

CHRISTMAS *Party Planner*

LOCATION:

DATE:

TIME:

NO. OF GUESTS

BUDGET:

THEME

DRESS CODE

KIDS INVITE
◯ YES ◯ NO

SCHEDULE

TO-DOS
☐
☐
☐
☐
☐
☐
☐
☐
☐
☐
☐
☐
☐
☐

ACTIVITIES / GAMES
◯
◯
◯
◯
◯
◯

ROLES

CHRISTMAS *Party Planner*

LOCATION: **DATE:**

TIME: **NO. OF GUESTS**   **BUDGET:**

THEME	DRESS CODE	KIDS INVITE
		YES NO

SCHEDULE	TO-DOS
	☐
	☐
	☐
	☐
	☐
	☐
	☐
	☐
	☐
	☐
	☐
	☐
	☐
	☐

ACTIVITIES / GAMES   **ROLES**

CHRISTMAS *Party Planner*

LOCATION:

DATE:

TIME:

NO. OF GUESTS

BUDGET:

THEME	DRESS CODE	KIDS INVITE
		◯ YES ◯ NO

SCHEDULE

TO-DOS

☐
☐
☐
☐
☐
☐
☐
☐
☐
☐
☐
☐
☐
☐

ACTIVITIES / GAMES

ROLES

CHRISTMAS *Party Planner*

LOCATION:

DATE:

TIME:

NO. OF GUESTS

BUDGET:

THEME	DRESS CODE	KIDS INVITE
		YES NO

SCHEDULE

TO-DOS

- [ ]
- [ ]
- [ ]
- [ ]
- [ ]
- [ ]
- [ ]
- [ ]
- [ ]
- [ ]
- [ ]
- [ ]
- [ ]
- [ ]
- [ ]

ACTIVITIES / GAMES

ROLES

CHRISTMAS *Party Planner*

LOCATION:

DATE:

TIME:

NO. OF GUESTS

BUDGET:

THEME	DRESS CODE	KIDS INVITE
		◯ YES ◯ NO

SCHEDULE

TO-DOS

☐
☐
☐
☐
☐
☐
☐
☐
☐
☐
☐
☐
☐
☐

ACTIVITIES / GAMES

ROLES

CHRISTMAS *Party Planner*

LOCATION:

DATE:

TIME:

NO. OF GUESTS

BUDGET:

THEME

DRESS CODE

KIDS INVITE

◯ YES ◯ NO

SCHEDULE

TO-DOS

- [ ]
- [ ]
- [ ]
- [ ]
- [ ]
- [ ]
- [ ]
- [ ]
- [ ]
- [ ]
- [ ]
- [ ]
- [ ]

ACTIVITIES / GAMES

ROLES

CHRISTMAS *Party Planner*

LOCATION: DATE:

TIME: NO. OF GUESTS   BUDGET:

THEME	DRESS CODE	KIDS INVITE
		○ YES ○ NO

SCHEDULE

TO-DOS

- ☐
- ☐
- ☐
- ☐
- ☐
- ☐
- ☐
- ☐
- ☐
- ☐
- ☐
- ☐
- ☐

ACTIVITIES / GAMES

ROLES

CHRISTMAS *Party Planner*

LOCATION:

DATE:

TIME:

NO. OF GUESTS

BUDGET:

THEME

DRESS CODE

KIDS INVITE

YES   NO

SCHEDULE

TO-DOS

- [ ]
- [ ]
- [ ]
- [ ]
- [ ]
- [ ]
- [ ]
- [ ]
- [ ]
- [ ]
- [ ]
- [ ]
- [ ]
- [ ]

ACTIVITIES / GAMES

ROLES

CHRISTMAS *Party Planner*

LOCATION:

DATE:

TIME:

NO. OF GUESTS

BUDGET:

THEME

DRESS CODE

KIDS INVITE

○ YES ○ NO

SCHEDULE

TO-DOS

☐
☐
☐
☐
☐
☐
☐
☐
☐
☐
☐
☐
☐

ACTIVITIES / GAMES

ROLES

CHRISTMAS *Party Planner*

LOCATION: **DATE:**

TIME: **NO. OF GUESTS**   **BUDGET:**

THEME   **DRESS CODE**   **KIDS INVITE**

YES   NO

SCHEDULE

TO-DOS

- [ ]
- [ ]
- [ ]
- [ ]
- [ ]
- [ ]
- [ ]
- [ ]
- [ ]
- [ ]
- [ ]
- [ ]
- [ ]

ACTIVITIES / GAMES

ROLES

CHRISTMAS *Party Planner*

LOCATION:

DATE:

TIME:

NO. OF GUESTS

BUDGET:

THEME

DRESS CODE

KIDS INVITE

◯ YES ◯ NO

SCHEDULE

TO-DOS

☐
☐
☐
☐
☐
☐
☐
☐
☐
☐
☐
☐
☐

ACTIVITIES / GAMES

ROLES

CHRISTMAS *Party Planner*

LOCATION:

DATE:

TIME:

NO. OF GUESTS

BUDGET:

THEME

DRESS CODE

KIDS INVITE

YES   NO

SCHEDULE

TO-DOS

☐
☐
☐
☐
☐
☐
☐
☐
☐
☐
☐
☐
☐
☐

ACTIVITIES / GAMES

ROLES

CHRISTMAS *Party Planner*

LOCATION:

DATE:

TIME:

NO. OF GUESTS

BUDGET:

THEME

DRESS CODE

KIDS INVITE

YES   NO

SCHEDULE

TO-DOS

- [ ]
- [ ]
- [ ]
- [ ]
- [ ]
- [ ]
- [ ]
- [ ]
- [ ]
- [ ]
- [ ]
- [ ]
- [ ]

ACTIVITIES / GAMES

ROLES

CHRISTMAS *Party Planner*

LOCATION: DATE:

TIME: NO. OF GUESTS   BUDGET:

THEME	DRESS CODE	KIDS INVITE
		YES NO

SCHEDULE	TO-DOS
	☐
	☐
	☐
	☐
	☐
	☐
	☐
	☐
	☐
	☐
	☐
	☐
	☐
	☐

ACTIVITIES / GAMES   **ROLES**

CHRISTMAS *Party Planner*

LOCATION:

DATE:

TIME:

NO. OF GUESTS

BUDGET:

THEME

DRESS CODE

KIDS INVITE

YES   NO

SCHEDULE

TO-DOS

- ☐
- ☐
- ☐
- ☐
- ☐
- ☐
- ☐
- ☐
- ☐
- ☐
- ☐
- ☐
- ☐

ACTIVITIES / GAMES

ROLES

CHRISTMAS *Party Planner*

LOCATION: DATE:

TIME: NO. OF GUESTS   BUDGET:

THEME   DRESS CODE   KIDS INVITE

                                              YES   NO

SCHEDULE		TO-DOS	
		☐	
		☐	
		☐	
		☐	
		☐	
		☐	
		☐	
		☐	
		☐	
		☐	
		☐	
		☐	
		☐	
		☐	

ACTIVITIES / GAMES   ROLES

CHRISTMAS *Party Planner*

LOCATION:

DATE:

TIME:

NO. OF GUESTS

BUDGET:

THEME

DRESS CODE

KIDS INVITE

YES   NO

SCHEDULE

TO-DOS

ACTIVITIES / GAMES

ROLES

CHRISTMAS *Party Planner*

LOCATION:

DATE:

TIME:

NO. OF GUESTS

BUDGET:

THEME

DRESS CODE

KIDS INVITE

YES   NO

SCHEDULE

TO-DOS

☐
☐
☐
☐
☐
☐
☐
☐
☐
☐
☐
☐
☐
☐

ACTIVITIES / GAMES

ROLES

CHRISTMAS *Party Planner*

LOCATION:

DATE:

TIME:

NO. OF GUESTS

BUDGET:

THEME

DRESS CODE

KIDS INVITE

YES ⚪ NO ⚪

SCHEDULE

TO-DOS

☐
☐
☐
☐
☐
☐
☐
☐
☐
☐
☐
☐
☐

ACTIVITIES / GAMES

ROLES

CHRISTMAS *Party Planner*

LOCATION:

DATE:

TIME:

NO. OF GUESTS

BUDGET:

THEME

DRESS CODE

KIDS INVITE

YES   NO

SCHEDULE

TO-DOS

☐
☐
☐
☐
☐
☐
☐
☐
☐
☐
☐
☐
☐
☐

ACTIVITIES / GAMES

ROLES

CHRISTMAS *Party Planner*

LOCATION: **DATE:**

TIME: **NO. OF GUESTS**   **BUDGET:**

THEME	DRESS CODE	KIDS INVITE
		YES NO

SCHEDULE

TO-DOS

- [ ]
- [ ]
- [ ]
- [ ]
- [ ]
- [ ]
- [ ]
- [ ]
- [ ]
- [ ]
- [ ]
- [ ]
- [ ]

ACTIVITIES / GAMES

ROLES

CHRISTMAS *Party Planner*

LOCATION:

DATE:

TIME:

NO. OF GUESTS

BUDGET:

THEME

DRESS CODE

KIDS INVITE

YES   NO

SCHEDULE	

ACTIVITIES / GAMES

TO-DOS

☐
☐
☐
☐
☐
☐
☐
☐
☐
☐
☐
☐
☐
☐

ROLES

CHRISTMAS *Party Planner*

LOCATION:

DATE:

TIME:

NO. OF GUESTS

BUDGET:

THEME

DRESS CODE

KIDS INVITE

YES   NO

SCHEDULE

TO-DOS

☐
☐
☐
☐
☐
☐
☐
☐
☐
☐
☐
☐
☐

ACTIVITIES / GAMES

ROLES

CHRISTMAS *Party Planner*

LOCATION: DATE:

TIME: NO. OF GUESTS   BUDGET:

THEME   DRESS CODE   KIDS INVITE

                                              YES   NO

SCHEDULE

TO-DOS
☐
☐
☐
☐
☐
☐
☐
☐
☐
☐
☐
☐

ACTIVITIES / GAMES   ROLES

CHRISTMAS *Party Planner*

LOCATION:

DATE:

TIME:

NO. OF GUESTS

BUDGET:

THEME	DRESS CODE	KIDS INVITE
		○ YES NO

SCHEDULE

TO-DOS

☐
☐
☐
☐
☐
☐
☐
☐
☐
☐
☐
☐
☐

ACTIVITIES / GAMES

ROLES

CHRISTMAS *Party Planner*

LOCATION: DATE:

TIME: NO. OF GUESTS   BUDGET:

THEME   DRESS CODE   KIDS INVITE

                                                   YES   NO

SCHEDULE	TO-DOS
	☐
	☐
	☐
	☐
	☐
	☐
	☐
	☐
	☐
	☐
	☐
	☐
	☐

ACTIVITIES / GAMES   ROLES

CHRISTMAS *Party Planner*

LOCATION:

DATE:

TIME:

NO. OF GUESTS

BUDGET:

THEME	DRESS CODE	KIDS INVITE
		◯ YES ◯ NO

SCHEDULE

TO-DOS

☐
☐
☐
☐
☐
☐
☐
☐
☐
☐
☐
☐
☐

ACTIVITIES / GAMES

ROLES

CHRISTMAS *Party Planner*

LOCATION:

DATE:

TIME:

NO. OF GUESTS

BUDGET:

THEME

DRESS CODE

KIDS INVITE

YES   NO

SCHEDULE		TO-DOS	
		☐	
		☐	
		☐	
		☐	
		☐	
		☐	
		☐	
		☐	
		☐	
		☐	
		☐	
		☐	
		☐	

ACTIVITIES / GAMES

ROLES

CHRISTMAS *Party Planner*

LOCATION:

DATE:

TIME:

NO. OF GUESTS

BUDGET:

THEME

DRESS CODE

KIDS INVITE

○ YES ○ NO

SCHEDULE

TO-DOS

- ☐
- ☐
- ☐
- ☐
- ☐
- ☐
- ☐
- ☐
- ☐
- ☐
- ☐
- ☐
- ☐
- ☐

ACTIVITIES / GAMES

ROLES

CHRISTMAS *Party Planner*

LOCATION: DATE:

TIME: NO. OF GUESTS   BUDGET:

THEME   DRESS CODE   KIDS INVITE

                                                   YES   NO

SCHEDULE	TO-DOS
	☐
	☐
	☐
	☐
	☐
	☐
	☐
	☐
	☐
	☐
	☐
	☐
	☐
	☐

ACTIVITIES / GAMES   ROLES

CHRISTMAS *Party Planner*

LOCATION: DATE:

TIME: NO. OF GUESTS BUDGET:

THEME DRESS CODE KIDS INVITE

YES NO

SCHEDULE

TO-DOS

☐
☐
☐
☐
☐
☐
☐
☐
☐
☐
☐
☐
☐
☐

ACTIVITIES / GAMES

ROLES

CHRISTMAS *Party Planner*

LOCATION: DATE:

TIME: NO. OF GUESTS   BUDGET:

THEME   DRESS CODE   KIDS INVITE

                                                YES   NO

SCHEDULE	TO-DOS
	☐
	☐
	☐
	☐
	☐
	☐
	☐
	☐
	☐
	☐
	☐
	☐
	☐

ACTIVITIES / GAMES   ROLES

CHRISTMAS *Party Planner*

LOCATION:

DATE:

TIME:

NO. OF GUESTS

BUDGET:

THEME

DRESS CODE

KIDS INVITE

YES   NO

SCHEDULE

TO-DOS

- [ ]
- [ ]
- [ ]
- [ ]
- [ ]
- [ ]
- [ ]
- [ ]
- [ ]
- [ ]
- [ ]
- [ ]
- [ ]

ACTIVITIES / GAMES

ROLES

CHRISTMAS *Party Planner*

LOCATION: **DATE:**

TIME: **NO. OF GUESTS**   **BUDGET:**

THEME   **DRESS CODE**   **KIDS INVITE**

                                             YES   NO

SCHEDULE

TO-DOS

- [ ]
- [ ]
- [ ]
- [ ]
- [ ]
- [ ]
- [ ]
- [ ]
- [ ]
- [ ]
- [ ]
- [ ]
- [ ]
- [ ]

ACTIVITIES / GAMES   **ROLES**

CHRISTMAS *Party Planner*

LOCATION: **DATE:**

TIME: **NO. OF GUESTS**   **BUDGET:**

THEME	DRESS CODE	KIDS INVITE
		◯ YES ◯ NO

SCHEDULE

TO-DOS

☐
☐
☐
☐
☐
☐
☐
☐
☐
☐
☐
☐
☐

ACTIVITIES / GAMES

ROLES

CHRISTMAS *Party Planner*

LOCATION: DATE:

TIME: NO. OF GUESTS   BUDGET:

THEME   DRESS CODE   KIDS INVITE

                                                       YES   NO

SCHEDULE		TO-DOS	
		☐	
		☐	
		☐	
		☐	
		☐	
		☐	
		☐	
		☐	
		☐	
		☐	
		☐	
		☐	
		☐	

         ACTIVITIES / GAMES   **ROLES**

CHRISTMAS *Party Planner*

LOCATION: DATE:

TIME: NO. OF GUESTS   BUDGET:

THEME	DRESS CODE	KIDS INVITE
		◯ YES ◯ NO

SCHEDULE

TO-DOS

☐
☐
☐
☐
☐
☐
☐
☐
☐
☐
☐
☐
☐
☐

ACTIVITIES / GAMES

ROLES

CHRISTMAS *Party Planner*

LOCATION: DATE:

TIME: NO. OF GUESTS BUDGET:

THEME DRESS CODE KIDS INVITE

YES   NO

SCHEDULE	TO-DOS
	☐
	☐
	☐
	☐
	☐
	☐
	☐
	☐
	☐
	☐
	☐
	☐
	☐

ACTIVITIES / GAMES   ROLES

CHRISTMAS *Party Planner*

LOCATION:

DATE:

TIME:

NO. OF GUESTS

BUDGET:

THEME	DRESS CODE	KIDS INVITE
		YES NO

SCHEDULE

TO-DOS

- [ ]
- [ ]
- [ ]
- [ ]
- [ ]
- [ ]
- [ ]
- [ ]
- [ ]
- [ ]
- [ ]
- [ ]
- [ ]

ACTIVITIES / GAMES

ROLES

CHRISTMAS *Party Planner*

LOCATION: DATE:

TIME: NO. OF GUESTS   BUDGET:

THEME   DRESS CODE   KIDS INVITE

YES   NO

SCHEDULE		TO-DOS	
		☐	
		☐	
		☐	
		☐	
		☐	
		☐	
		☐	
		☐	
		☐	
		☐	
		☐	
		☐	
		☐	

ACTIVITIES / GAMES   ROLES